The STRANGEST Plants on Earth

MEAT-EATING PLANTS

Margee Gould

PowerKiDS
press
New York

Published in 2012 by The Rosen Publishing Group, Inc.
29 East 21st Street, New York, NY 10010

First Edition

Editor: Jennifer Way
Book Design: Ashley Drago

Photo Credits: Cover Jupiterimages/Photos.com/Thinkstock; pp. 4–5 (main), 9, 13, 21 iStockphoto/ Thinkstock; p. 4 (inset) © www.iStockphoto.com/Ryan Poling; pp. 6, 8, 14, 17 Shutterstock.com; p. 7 (left) © www.iStockphoto.com/Pawel Burgiel; p. 7 (right) © www.iStockphoto.com/Denice Breaux; p. 10 © www.iStockphoto.com/Jonathan Maddock; p. 11 Altrendo Nature/Getty Images; p. 12 Universal Images Group/Getty Images; p. 15 Hemera/Thinkstock; p. 16 David Cavagnaro/ Getty Images; p. 18 © A. Jagel/age fotostock; p. 19 Carole Drake/Getty Images; p. 20 (main) Oxford Scientific/Getty Images; p. 20 (inset) Dr. Fred Hossler/Getty Images.

Library of Congress Cataloging-in-Publication Data

Gould, Margee.
    Meat-eating plants / by Margee Gould. — 1st ed.
        p. cm. — (The strangest plants on Earth)
    Includes index.
    ISBN 978-1-4488-4988-8 (library binding)
    1. Carnivorous plants—Juvenile literature. I. Title. II. Series: Strangest plants on Earth.
    QK917.G68 2012
    583'.75—dc22

2010047870

Manufactured in the United States of America

CPSIA Compliance Information: Batch #WS11PK: For Further Information contact Rosen Publishing, New York, New York at 1-800-237-9932

Contents

Did You Say Meat-Eating?

What do you know about plants? Do you know that plants need sunlight, water, and rich soil to be healthy? Plants use these basic things to make their own food.

What happens if the soil does not give a plant enough **nutrients**, though? Some plants have **adapted** strange ways to get the nutrients they need to grow. Some plants eat meat! Plants such as the Venus flytrap catch and digest bugs. Let's find out more about these leafy **carnivores**.

The Venus flytrap, shown here, has leaves that snap shut to trap bugs.

This fly is trapped on a sundew plant's sticky leaf. The leaf will curl around the fly and the plant will digest its meal.

The Venus flytrap flowers in the spring. The flowers are shown here.

It's Alive!

Just as many plants do, meat-eating plants have roots, stems, leaves, and flowering parts. All these parts work together and use the Sun to make food for the plant. Meat-eating plants have adapted to eating meat to get nutrients that the soil lacks. Meat-eating plants have parts such as sharp or sticky hairs and slippery leaves to help them catch food.

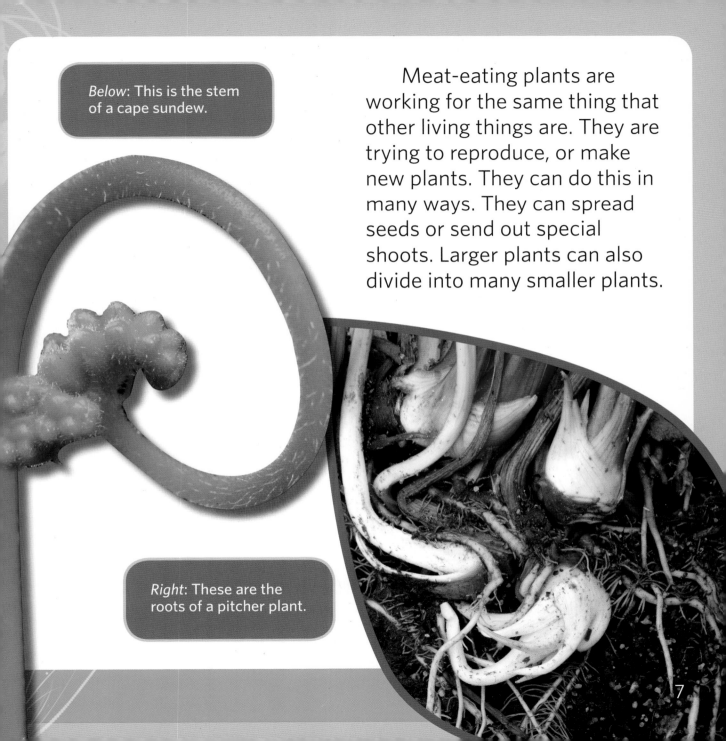

Below: This is the stem of a cape sundew.

Meat-eating plants are working for the same thing that other living things are. They are trying to reproduce, or make new plants. They can do this in many ways. They can spread seeds or send out special shoots. Larger plants can also divide into many smaller plants.

Right: These are the roots of a pitcher plant.

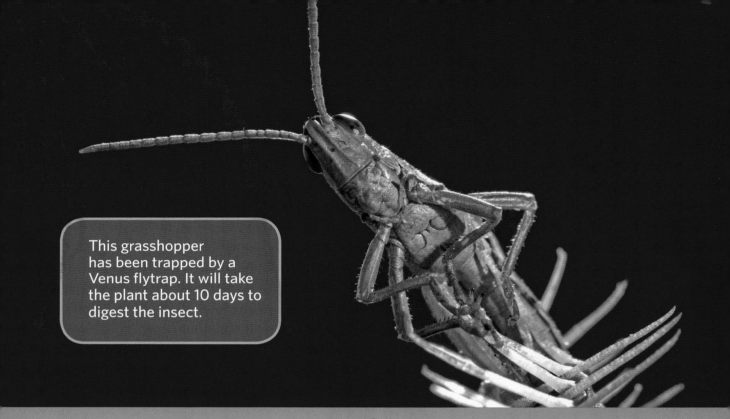

This grasshopper has been trapped by a Venus flytrap. It will take the plant about 10 days to digest the insect.

How Do They Do It?

You might wonder how a plant can eat another living thing. Plants do not have teeth, throats, or stomachs. Most meat-eating plants put out a watery material called **digestive fluid**. This fluid breaks down food, as the **acid** does in our stomachs. It breaks down the insect, leaving just the outer skeleton.

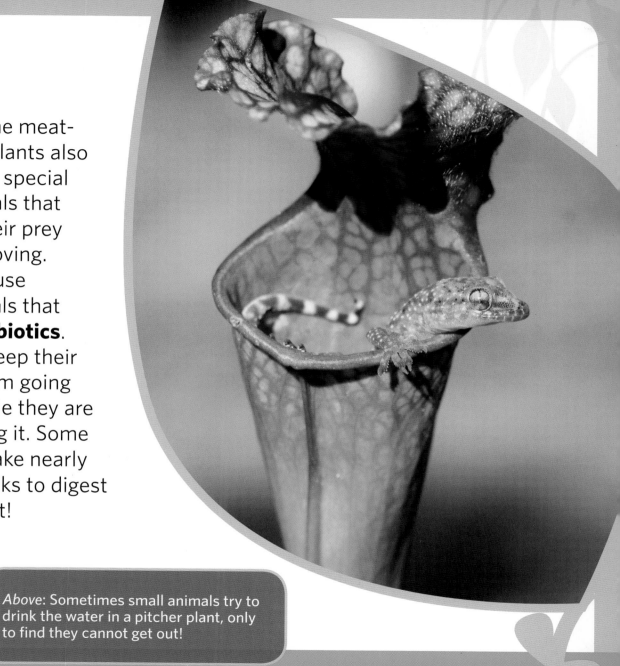

Some meat-eating plants also give out special chemicals that keep their prey from moving. Others use chemicals that are **antibiotics**. These keep their food from going bad while they are digesting it. Some plants take nearly two weeks to digest an insect!

Above: Sometimes small animals try to drink the water in a pitcher plant, only to find they cannot get out!

At Home in the Swamp

Meat-eating plants live on every continent on Earth except Antarctica. They can be found high up on mountainsides, along **coastal plains**, or in **rain forests**.

The place where a plant or animal lives is called its habitat. No matter where in the world

they are, almost all meat-eating plant habitats are wet, swampy lands with soil that does not have a lot of nutrients. All plants need **nitrogen** to live. Nitrogen is a gas that makes plants able to grow and thrive. Watery soil has little nitrogen. The water carries it away. Luckily for meat-eating plants, there is plenty of nitrogen in insects and other animals.

Above: These yellow trumpet pitcher plants are growing in a swampy area in Georgia.

Who Grows That?

People around the world grow meat-eating plants in their homes or in greenhouses. Some meat-eating plant **species** would be **extinct** if it were not for these people.

However, people's interest in these plants has caused them problems, too. People take these plants from the wild to grow them at home. This is why so many of these plants are endangered now. Many species of meat-eating plants are on the **endangered species list**. In fact, around 27 species are listed as in trouble.

Above: Meat-eating plants, such as these pitcher plants, are sometimes grown at special gardens people can visit. These are called botanical gardens.

Meet the Venus Flytrap

The Venus flytrap is a famous insect-eating plant. In the wild, it lives in only a few swampy places in North Carolina and South Carolina. It is also grown in greenhouses.

Each of the Venus flytrap's leaves has two parts, or lobes. These lobes have fine hairs on

them. If an insect touches these hairs as it lands on the leaf, the two parts of the leaves snap together.

Once a bug is trapped inside, the lobes put out digestive fluid. It takes the Venus flytrap up to 10 days to digest an insect. Then it pops open and is ready for its next meal!

Above: The Venus flytrap is listed as vulnerable. This means that it is almost endangered.

The Deadly Pitcher Plant

Pitcher plants are named for their pitcher-shaped leaves. These leaves hold water just as a pitcher in your kitchen might. Some pitcher plants are only about 4 inches (10 cm) tall. Others can grow as tall as 4 feet (1 m). Pitcher plants also come in many colors, including green, yellow, white, and red.

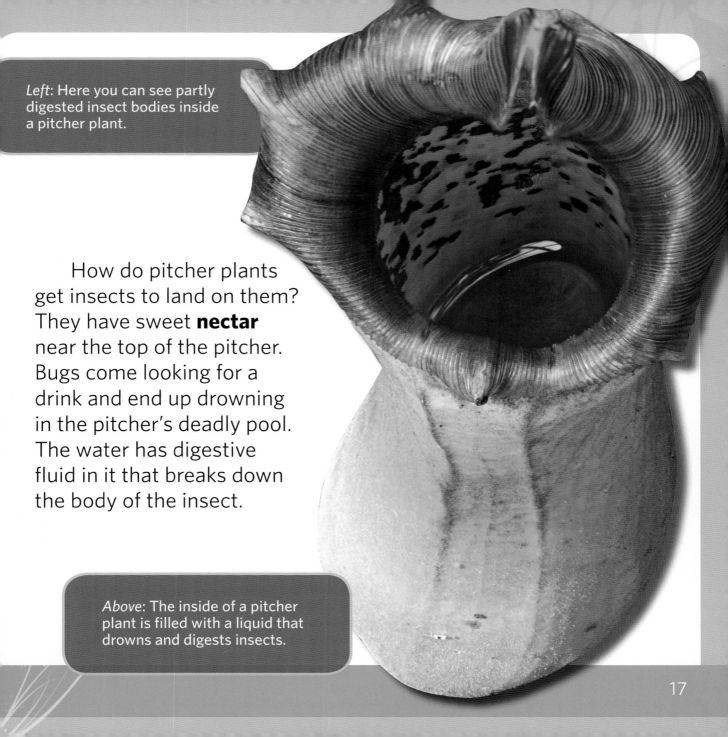

Left: Here you can see partly digested insect bodies inside a pitcher plant.

How do pitcher plants get insects to land on them? They have sweet **nectar** near the top of the pitcher. Bugs come looking for a drink and end up drowning in the pitcher's deadly pool. The water has digestive fluid in it that breaks down the body of the insect.

Above: The inside of a pitcher plant is filled with a liquid that drowns and digests insects.

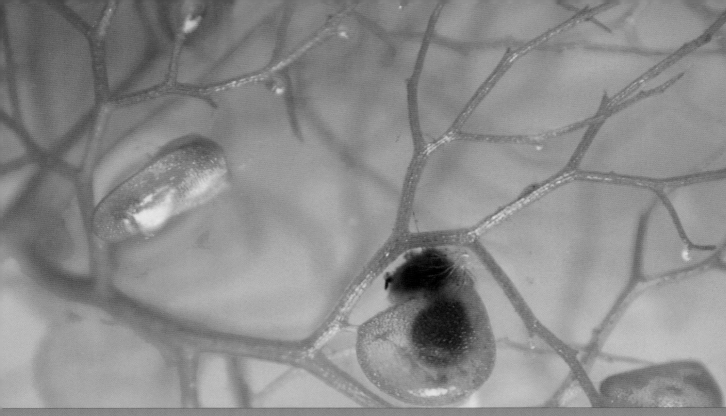

The Strange Bladderwort

The bladderwort is truly a strange plant! This meat-eating plant can be found in the water of ponds or swamps. It can also be found under damp, sandy soil. Some bladderworts even live in the wet, rotting bark of trees. Bladderworts are rootless plants. They are covered in featherlike branches.

Their stems are covered in hundreds or thousands of clear bags, called bladders. These bags are each about the size of a pinhead. Do not let their tiny size fool you, though. Each of these tiny bags is a lightning-quick trap for insects or small underwater animals.

Above: A bladderwort's flowers are the only part of the plant that is above the water or soil.

Stuck on You, Sundew

Picture a plant that sparkles like a diamond. It has a beautiful, sweet smell, too. If you were an insect, you might want to stop by this plant for a drink of nectar. Watch out, though! Once you land on a sundew, you will be staying for lunch. Too bad for you that insects are the main course!

Left: This ant is trapped on the shiny, sticky hairs of a sundew. *Inset*: This is a close-up look at the hairs of a sundew plant.

Each sundew leaf has about 250 hairs on it. Each hair has a drop of sticky liquid on its tip. These gluelike drops trap insects that land on the leaves. The sundew leaves may even curl around the insect. More sticky glue covers it. Soon the bug cannot breathe and dies. The sundew will now digest it and wait for its next meal.

Above: This moth is stuck on a sundew. Soon the plant's sticky leaves will curl around the insect and digest it.

21

1. Some pitcher plants make a special chemical that keeps an insect from moving once it has tasted the nectar.

2. The Venus flytrap closes on an insect only if two hairs are touched at the same time.

3. There are about 220 species of bladderworts. There are more species of bladderworts than of any other meat-eating plant.

4. Some Venus flytraps can live up to 30 years!

5. Mosquitoes often lay their eggs in pitcher plant pools. The digestive fluid does not hurt the eggs!

It's a Fact!

6. The king sundew grows in South Africa. It has leaves that are 2 feet (61 cm) long!

7. Tropical pitcher plants are some of the largest in the world. Their vines can reach 50 feet (15 m) in length and their pitchers are about 1 to 4 feet (.3–1.2 m) tall.

8. People in Southeast Asia have been known to use tropical pitcher plant vines as ropes!

Glossary

acid (A-sud) Something that breaks down matter faster than water does.

adapted (uh-DAPT-ed) Changed to fit requirements.

antibiotics (an-tee-by-AH-tiks) Things that kill bacteria.

carnivores (KAHR-neh-vorz) Things that eat animals.

coastal plains (KOHS-tul PLAYNZ) Places with flat, low land near seacoasts.

digestive fluid (dy-JES-tiv FLOO-ud) Watery matter that helps break down food into energy.

endangered species list (in-DAYN-jerd SPEE-sheez LIST) A list of species that will likely die out if we do not protect them.

extinct (ik-STINGKT) No longer existing.

nectar (NEK-tur) A sweet liquid found in flowers.

nitrogen (NY-truh-jen) A gas without taste, color, or odor that can be found in the soil.

nutrients (NOO-tree-ents) Food that a living thing needs to live and grow.

rain forests (RAYN FOR-ests) Thick forests that receive a large amount of rain during the year.

species (SPEE-sheez) One kind of living thing. All people are one species.

Index

B

bug(s), 4, 15, 17, 21

C

coastal plains, 10

D

digestive fluid, 8, 15,
    17, 22

F

food, 4, 6, 8–9

H

hairs, 6, 14–15, 21–22

L

leaves, 6, 14–16, 21–22

N

nectar, 17, 20, 22

nitrogen, 11

P

people, 12–13, 22

R

rain forests, 10

roots, 6

S

seeds, 7

shoots, 7

soil, 4, 6, 11, 18

stems, 6, 19

Sun, 6

sunlight, 4

Web Sites

Due to the changing nature of Internet links, PowerKids
Press has developed an online list of Web sites related
to the subject of this book. This site is updated regularly.
Please use this link to access the list:
www.powerkidslinks.com/spe/meatplnt/